Maths
made easy

Key Stage 2
ages 9-11
Decimals

Author Peter Gash and David Clemson

Certificate

Congratulations to ....
(write your name here)
for successfully finishing this book.

☆ *You're a star!* ☆

DK

LONDON • NEW YORK • MUNICH • MELBOURNE • DELHI

Digit value

In the number 15.7, the digit 1 stands for a ten, the digit 5 for 5 units and the digit 7 for 7 tenths.

Write the values of the circled digits in these numbers.

2 2.⑦ [   ]   1②.9 [   ]

1③.6 [   ]   ④8.3 [   ]

③5.8 [   ]   2 5.⑤ [   ]

7②.4 [   ]   5⑨.2 [   ]

②2.7 [   ]   1 2.⑨ [   ]

1 3.⑥ [   ]   4⑧.3 [   ]

3⑤.8 [   ]   ②5.5 [   ]

⑦2.4 [   ]   5 9.② [   ]

6 9.① [   ]   ③2.4 [   ]

Digit value

Write the values of the circled digits in these numbers.

3 3 . (8)   [   ]   2(3) . 1   [   ]

2(4) . 7   [   ]   (5)9 . 4   [   ]

(4)6 . 9   [   ]   3 7 . (6)   [   ]

8(3) . 5   [   ]   6(0) . 3   [   ]

(1)4 . 9   [   ]   3 1 . (8)   [   ]

1 4 . (7)   [   ]   6(9) . 4   [   ]

5(7) . 2   [   ]   (4)7 . 6   [   ]

(9)1 . 3   [   ]   7 1 . (5)   [   ]

5 9 . (9)   [   ]   3(6) . 4   [   ]

4(7) . 3   [   ]   (7)2 . 7   [   ]

Hundredths

Another way of writing $^{25}/_{100}$ is as a decimal.

$$^{25}/_{100} = 0.25 \qquad ^{35}/_{100} = 0.35 \qquad ^{45}/_{100} = 0.45 \text{ and so on.}$$

$1^{4}/_{100}$ is written 1.04 as a decimal. The 0 fills the space when there are no tenths.

Write these numbers as decimals.

$1^{29}/_{100}$ ☐ $4^{58}/_{100}$ ☐

$7^{47}/_{100}$ ☐ $3^{10}/_{100}$ ☐

$4^{31}/_{100}$ ☐ $7^{9}/_{100}$ ☐

$5^{24}/_{100}$ ☐ $2^{36}/_{100}$ ☐

$8^{67}/_{100}$ ☐ $4^{85}/_{100}$ ☐

$2^{33}/_{100}$ ☐ $8^{99}/_{100}$ ☐

$6^{45}/_{100}$ ☐ $3^{6}/_{100}$ ☐

$9^{75}/_{100}$ ☐ $5^{18}/_{100}$ ☐

$1^{58}/_{100}$ ☐ $6^{2}/_{100}$ ☐

Hundredths

Write these numbers as decimals.

$4\frac{79}{100}$ ☐ $6\frac{14}{100}$ ☐

$4\frac{78}{100}$ ☐ $2\frac{68}{100}$ ☐

$2\frac{41}{100}$ ☐ $\frac{7}{100}$ ☐

$8\frac{6}{100}$ ☐ $\frac{9}{100}$ ☐

$7\frac{34}{100}$ ☐ $5\frac{54}{100}$ ☐

$7\frac{33}{100}$ ☐ $2\frac{21}{100}$ ☐

$1\frac{79}{100}$ ☐ $2\frac{87}{100}$ ☐

$\frac{98}{100}$ ☐ $8\frac{21}{100}$ ☐

$4\frac{44}{100}$ ☐ $8\frac{66}{100}$ ☐

$6\frac{39}{100}$ ☐ $4\frac{12}{100}$ ☐

$9\frac{51}{100}$ ☐ $1\frac{11}{100}$ ☐

Hundredths

In the number 25.68, the digit 2 stands for 2 tens, the digit 5 for 5 units, the digit 6 for 6 tenths, and the digit 8 for 8 hundredths.

Write the values of the circled digits.

35.8⑥ [   ]   4⑤.05 [   ]

1⑦.78 [   ]   ⑥8.34 [   ]

⑤8.93 [   ]   79.5③ [   ]

83.4④ [   ]   6①.23 [   ]

⑨2.84 [   ]   83.⑤1 [   ]

24.7⑧ [   ]   59.4⑥ [   ]

4⑥.90 [   ]   ③7.69 [   ]

72.4① [   ]   10.3⑦ [   ]

84.7⑤ [   ]   1②.91 [   ]

Decimals on a calculator

You will need a calculator. To change 5 to 50 in one operation you can do a multiplication.

$$5 \ \times \ 10 \ = \ 50$$

You can change 50 back to 5 by dividing.

$$50 \ \div \ 10 \ = \ 5$$

Write the multiplying or dividing operations you can use to change these numbers. Try them on your calculator. The first one has been done for you.

2 to 20	x 10	30 to 3	
50 to 5		7 to 70	
80 to 8		25 to 2.5	
4.2 to 42		9.5 to 95	
2.9 to 0.29		3.5 to 35	
1.05 to 10.5		40.7 to 4.07	
6.6 to 66		58 to 5.8	

Decimals on a calculator

Write the multiplying or dividing operations you can use to change these numbers. Try them on your calculator.

6 to 600		11 to 1.1	
100 to 10		3 to 30	
6.4 to 640		13.9 to 139	
4.2 to 0.42		5.75 to 575	
50 to 5000		8 to 0.08	
29 to 2.9		50 to 0.5	
8.6 to 86		47 to 470	
530 to 5.3		6 to 0.6	
2.9 to 29		4.16 to 416	
1000 to 10		250 to 25	

Decimals on a number line

You can show decimals on a number line. The arrow shows 1.3.

0   1   **1.3**   2

Draw arrows to show these decimals on the number lines.

0.3 and 1.5

0   1   2

0.9 and 1.7

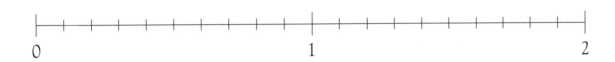

0   1   2

0.7 and 1.4

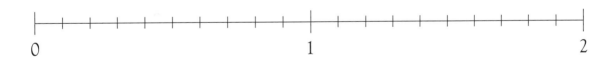

0   1   2

0.8 and 1.9

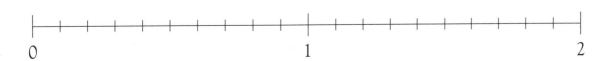

0   1   2

Decimals on a number line

You can show hundredths as decimals on a number line. The arrow shows 1.15.

Draw arrows to show these decimals on the number lines.

1.4, 1.65, and 1.95

3.45, 3.55, and 3.8

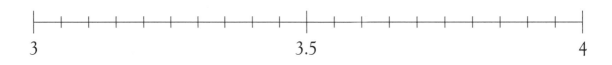

5.3, 5.35, and 5.85

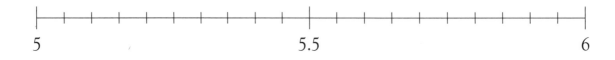

2.1, 2.25, and 2.75

Money

You can write amounts of money like decimals. There are 100p in £1, so you can write it as £1.00. You can write 105p as £1.05.

Write these amounts of money like decimals.

486p [ ]

912p [ ]

456p [ ]

103p [ ]

510p [ ]

8p [ ]

705p [ ]

999p [ ]

7p [ ]

89p [ ]

75p [ ]

570p [ ]

2p [ ]

415p [ ]

59p [ ]

45p [ ]

133p [ ]

1250p [ ]

1035p [ ]

1009p [ ]

Measurements as decimals

You can write measurements using a decimal point.

It is used to separate whole metres from centimetres: 125 cm = 1.25 m

or whole kilometres from metres: 4270 m = 4.27 km

or whole kilograms from grams: 750 g = 3.75 kg

or whole litres from millilitres: 5250 ml = 5.25 litres

Write these measurements like decimals.

150 cm [ ] m   1750 g [ ] kg

1500 ml [ ] litres   1250 m [ ] km

575 cm [ ] m   45 cm [ ] m

2200 ml [ ] litres   3950 g [ ] kg

1450 m [ ] km   1760 m [ ] km

3900 ml [ ] litres   5500 g [ ] kg

195 cm [ ] m   500 g [ ] kg

2350 g [ ] kg   6750 m [ ] km

Rounding

When rounding decimals to the nearest whole number, numbers ending in 0.50 or more are *rounded up*. Numbers ending in 0.49 or less are *rounded down*.

2.48 rounds down to 2, and 3.75 rounds up to 4.

Round these decimals up or down to the nearest whole number.

4.29 ☐   7.86 ☐

6.57 ☐   59.45 ☐

7.43 ☐   42.71 ☐

18.2 ☐   91.93 ☐

52.1 ☐   62.78 ☐

8.85 ☐   13.64 ☐

9.01 ☐   26.01 ☐

5.63 ☐   35.55 ☐

Rounding

Round these amounts of money and measurements up or down to the nearest whole number.

£4.65 [ ]   8.65 kg [ ]

5.35 kg [ ]   £3.15 [ ]

£8.10 [ ]   6.3 m [ ]

7.75 cm [ ]   2.85 m [ ]

5.89 cm [ ]   £3.55 [ ]

£6.37 [ ]   9.45 kg [ ]

5.25 kg [ ]   4.1 m [ ]

£0.50 [ ]   8.88 kg [ ]

6.05 cm [ ]   £25.49 [ ]

Decimal equivalents

Write the decimal equivalents.

$\frac{8}{10}$ = ☐ $\frac{4}{10}$ = ☐

489p = ☐   35p = ☐

$\frac{1}{5}$ = ☐   35 cm = ☐

625 cm = ☐ $\frac{4}{5}$ = ☐

275p = ☐   150p = ☐

55 cm = ☐ $\frac{1}{10}$ = ☐

$\frac{2}{5}$ = ☐   280 cm = ☐

308p = ☐   16 cm = ☐

Decimals from fractions

Use your calculator to find the decimal equivalents of these fractions. Write the divisions you can use.

	Division	Answer			Division	Answer
$\frac{1}{100}$ =		=		$\frac{2}{10}$ =		=
$\frac{25}{100}$ =		=		$\frac{5}{100}$ =		=
$\frac{49}{100}$ =		=		$\frac{7}{10}$ =		=
$\frac{3}{4}$ =		=		$\frac{1}{4}$ =		=
$\frac{1}{2}$ =		=		$\frac{50}{100}$ =		=
$\frac{10}{100}$ =		=		$\frac{3}{60}$ =		=

Making an estimate

Write whether you would estimate the following to the nearest 10, 100, 1000, 10 000, 100 000 or 1 000 000.

The number of insects on Earth.

The number of children in a class.

The number of shops in a town.

The number of people watching a TV soap.

The number of spectators at an important football match.

The cost of a fleet of 15 cars (in pounds).

Give examples, similar to those above, of something that you might estimate to the nearest:

10

100

1000

10 000

100 000

1 000 000

Rounding to 100 and 1000

Round these numbers to the nearest 100 and then to the nearest 1000.

978

6829

3735

7511

2716

1008

Round the heights of these buildings to the nearest 100 cm.

  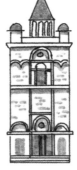 

12.76 m   36.17 m   22.98 m   18.22 m

Draw a ring around the option that shows the calculation in the box rounded to the nearest 1000.

1626 + 953

1500 + 1000

2000 + 1000

2500 + 900

5443 – 3771

5500 – 3500

6000 – 4000

5000 – 4000

Multiplying by 10

Multiply these decimals by 10.

0.25 ☐   3.14 ☐

1.75 ☐   15.27 ☐

5.56 ☐   156.35 ☐

These statues are one tenth of their real heights. Write their real heights.

32.8 mm   44.5 mm   22.6 mm

☐   ☐   ☐

Multiply each number on the left by 10 and draw a line to join it to the correct answer on the right.

1.25   7.3

0.19   35.8

3.58   5202.4

0.73   1.9

520.24   173.6

17.36   12.5

Multiplying by 10 and 100

Multiply these decimals by 100.

6.25 ☐   3.14 ☐

11.75 ☐   5.27 ☐

35.56 ☐   1506.25 ☐

Write the missing numbers in the boxes.

0.06 ☐   6

101.1   1011   ☐

0.09   0.9   ☐

13.26 ☐   ☐

3.145 ☐   ☐

Multiply each decimal on the left by 100 and draw a line to join it to the correct answer on the right.

1.35	1073
0.27	2736
0.027	5202.4
10.73	27
52.024	2.7
27.36	135

Decimal notation

You can write a decimal in words.

For example, 1.123 is one and one tenth, two hundredths and three thousandths.

Write out these decimals in words.

3.517

0.115

1.023

16.002

4.448

Decimal notation

Write the decimal equivalents for each of the following.

Three and six thousandths.

Box

One tenth, three hundredths and seven thousandths.

Box

Two tenths and five thousandths.

Box

Fifteen and three tenths, one hundredth and six thousandths.

Box

Nine tenths and nine thousandths.

Box

Twelve and one thousandth.

Box

One-step operations

You will need a calculator.
To change 2.5 to 25 in one operation you can do a multiplication.

$$2.5 \times 10 = 25$$

You can change 25 back to 2.5 by dividing.

$$25 \div 10 = 2.5$$

Similarly, you can change 2.5 to 250, and 250 back to 2.5 by multiplying and dividing by 100.

Write the one-step operation you can use to change these numbers. Try them on your calculator.

3.6 to 36 [ ]   15.2 to 1.52 [ ]

4.8 to 480 [ ]   250 to 2.5 [ ]

0.2 to 0.02 [ ]   0.01 to 1 [ ]

330 to 3.3 [ ]   990 to 9.9 [ ]

5 to 0.05 [ ]   0.3 to 3 [ ]

70 to 0.7 [ ]   5.5 to 550 [ ]

One-step operations

You will need a calculator.
To continue the pattern 2, 2.5, 3, 3.5, and so on, you can do an addition.

$$2 + 0.5 = 2.5 \quad 2.5 + 0.5 = 3 \quad 3 + 0.5 = 3.5 \text{ and so on.}$$

So the one step needed to continue the pattern is to add 0.5 each time.

Use a calculator to work out the one-step operation you can use to continue these patterns. Write the step.

1.82, 1.84, 1.86, and so on

0.09, 0.10, 0.11, and so on

5, 0.5, 0.05, and so on

0.16, 0.32, 0.64, and so on

1.55, 1.8, 2.05, and so on

0.064, 0.128, 0.256, and so on

Ordering decimals

Put these amounts in order from the largest to the smallest.

£3.56	£6.35	£3.65	£5.63	£5.36

12.65 km	16.25 km	15.26 km	15.62 km	12.56 litres

0.55 kg	0.09 kg	0.45 kg	0.54 kg	0.155 kg

Put these amounts in order from the smallest to the largest.

106p	£1.60	£0.95	97p	£1.65

1.35 m	110 cm	136 cm	1.53 m	1.01 m

1.25 litres	1200 ml	2.15 litres	1500 ml	1.56 litres

Converting

Convert these units.

2.125 km into m

15.15 km into m

6.05 km into m

7.005 km into m

7.255 kg into g

3.5 kg into g

7.155 kg into g

10.025 kg into g

1.25 litres into ml

10.25 litres into ml

0.755 litres into ml

1.055 litres into ml

Decimals on a number line

Write the decimal each arrow is pointing to.

Draw arrows to show these decimals on the number line: 1.1, 2.7, 1.5, 2.9, 2.1

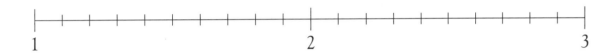

Write the decimal each arrow is pointing to.

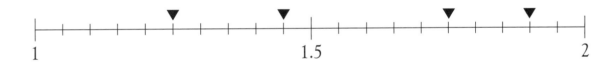

Draw arrows to show these decimals on the number line: 1.05, 1.55, 1.8, 1.35, 1.9

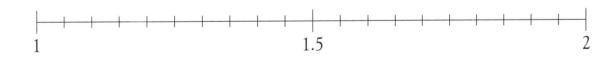

Write the decimal each arrow is pointing to.

Ordering decimals

Put these amounts in order from the largest to the smallest.

3.25	12.2	2.87	2.78	3.2

6.675	7.765	7.567	6.576	7.665

Put these amounts in order from the smallest to the largest.

1.75	1.57	2.05	2.15	2.005

16.681	18.616	16.816	18.661	18.166

Write the missing numbers to complete the sequences.

3.17		3.18
15.06		15.07
12.9		12.8
7.65		7.66
7.65		7.64

Word problems

	Answer	Working out
Add 2.3 litres and 450 ml.		
Add 375 ml and 5.25 litres.		
Subtract 255 g from 1.4 kg.		
Subtract 363 g from 2.59 kg.		

Solve these problems.

	Answer	Working out
A bag of nails weighs 1.25 kg and a small bag of screws weighs 225 g. What is the total weight of one bag of nails and two bags of screws?		
Andrew weighed some dried beans. They weighed 1.63 kg. He took 325 g of beans off the scales. What was the weight of the remaining beans?		
A measuring jug contained 1.75 litres of water. Sarah poured in another 355 ml. How much water was in the measuring jug?		
Indu made 1.85 litres of soup in a saucepan and then poured out two bowls, each of which took 325 ml. How much soup is left in the saucepan?		

Rounding

Round each decimal to the nearest whole number.

9.7 [ ]   10.3 [ ]

39.8 [ ]   14.5 [ ]

3.78 [ ]   14.33 [ ]

6.43 [ ]   18.05 [ ]

38.29 [ ]   156.82 [ ]

957.19 [ ]   100.95 [ ]

999.99 [ ]   101.01 [ ]

9.09 [ ]   110.11 [ ]

Rounding

Round each decimal to the nearest tenth.

3.28   ☐   2.83   ☐

9.47   ☐   12.53   ☐

12.59   ☐   111.51   ☐

111.15   ☐   17.12   ☐

17.17   ☐   2.58   ☐

1.53   ☐   8.96   ☐

1.99   ☐   22.07   ☐

24.25   ☐   5.55   ☐

100.01   ☐   19.89   ☐

Equivalents

Write the fraction or decimal equivalents.

$^7/_{10}$ ⬜

0.06 ⬜

0.003 ⬜

0.025 ⬜

$^{17}/_{100}$ ⬜

5.17 ⬜

6.25 ⬜

0.525 ⬜

4.205 ⬜

1.99 ⬜

1.09 ⬜

1.009 ⬜

9.09 ⬜

9.99 ⬜

Answer Section

Key Stage 2
Ages 9–11
Decimals

As your child finishes each page, check the answers together. Your child may like to stick a gold star at the top of each completed page as well as on the progress chart at the beginning of the book.

Digit value

In the number 15.7, the digit 1 stands for a ten, the digit 5 for 5 units and the digit 7 for 7 tenths.

Write the values of the circled digits in these numbers.

2 2.⑦	7 tenths		1②.9	2 units
1③.6	3 units		④8.3	4 tens
③5.8	3 tens		2 5.⑤	5 tenths
7②.4	2 units		5⑨.2	9 units
②2.7	2 tens		12.⑨	9 tenths
13.⑥	6 tenths		4⑧.3	8 units
3⑤.8	5 units		②5.5	2 tens
⑦2.4	7 tens		59.②	2 tenths
69.①	1 tenth		③2.4	3 tens

Digit value

Write the values of the circled digits in these numbers.

3 3.⑧	8 tenths		2③.1	3 units
2④.7	4 units		⑤9.4	5 tens
④6.9	4 tens		37.⑥	6 tenths
8③.5	3 units		6⓪.3	0 units
①4.9	1 ten		31.⑧	8 tenths
14.⑦	7 tenths		6⑨.4	9 units
5⑦.2	7 units		④7.6	4 tens
⑨1.3	9 tens		71.⑤	5 tenths
59.⑨	9 tenths		3⑥.4	6 units
4⑦.3	7 units		⑦2.7	7 tens

Hundredths

Another way of writing $\frac{25}{100}$ is as a decimal.

$$\frac{25}{100} = 0.25 \qquad \frac{35}{100} = 0.35 \qquad \frac{45}{100} = 0.45 \text{ and so on.}$$

$1\frac{4}{100}$ is written 1.04 as a decimal. The 0 fills the space when there are no tenths.

Write these numbers as decimals.

$1\frac{29}{100}$	1.29		$4\frac{58}{100}$	4.58
$7\frac{47}{100}$	7.47		$3\frac{10}{100}$	3.1
$4\frac{31}{100}$	4.31		$7\frac{9}{100}$	7.09
$5\frac{24}{100}$	5.24		$2\frac{36}{100}$	2.36
$8\frac{67}{100}$	8.67		$4\frac{85}{100}$	4.85
$2\frac{33}{100}$	2.33		$8\frac{99}{100}$	8.99
$6\frac{45}{100}$	6.45		$3\frac{6}{100}$	3.06
$9\frac{75}{100}$	9.75		$5\frac{18}{100}$	5.18
$1\frac{58}{100}$	1.58		$6\frac{2}{100}$	6.02

Hundredths

Write these numbers as decimals.

$4^{79}/_{100}$	4.79	$6^{14}/_{100}$	6.14
$4^{78}/_{100}$	4.78	$2^{68}/_{100}$	2.68
$2^{41}/_{100}$	2.41	$^{7}/_{100}$	0.07
$8^{6}/_{100}$	8.06	$^{9}/_{100}$	0.09
$7^{34}/_{100}$	7.34	$5^{54}/_{100}$	5.54
$7^{33}/_{100}$	7.33	$2^{21}/_{100}$	2.21
$1^{79}/_{100}$	1.79	$2^{87}/_{100}$	2.87
$^{98}/_{100}$	0.98	$8^{21}/_{100}$	8.21
$4^{44}/_{100}$	4.44	$8^{66}/_{100}$	8.66
$6^{39}/_{100}$	6.39	$4^{12}/_{100}$	4.12
$9^{51}/_{100}$	9.51	$1^{11}/_{100}$	1.11

Hundredths

In the number 25.68, the digit 2 stands for 2 tens, the digit 5 for 5 units, the digit 6 for 6 tenths and the digit 8 for 8 hundredths.

Write the values of the circled digits.

3 5.8⑥	6 hundredths	4⑤.05	5 units
1⑦.78	7 units	⑥8.34	6 tens
⑤8.93	5 tens	79.5③	3 hundredths
83.4④	4 hundredths	6①.23	1 unit
⑨2.84	9 tens	83.⑤1	5 tenths
2 4.7⑩	8 hundredths	59.4⑥	6 hundredths
4⑥.90	6 units	③7.69	3 tens
72.4①	1 hundredth	10.3⑦	7 hundredths
84.7⑤	5 hundredths	1②.91	2 units

Decimals on a calculator

You will need a calculator. To change 5 to 50 in one operation you can do a multiplication.

$$5 \times 10 = 50$$

You can change 50 back to 5 by dividing.

$$50 \div 10 = 5$$

Write the multiplying or dividing operations you can use to change these numbers. Try them on your calculator. The first one has been done for you.

2 to 20	x 10	30 to 3	÷ 10
50 to 5	÷ 10	7 to 70	x 10
80 to 8	÷ 10	25 to 2.5	÷ 10
4.2 to 42	x 10	9.5 to 95	x 10
2.9 to 0.29	÷ 10	3.5 to 35	x 10
1.05 to 10.5	x 10	40.7 to 4.07	÷ 10
6.6 to 66	x 10	58 to 5.8	÷ 10

Decimals on a calculator

Write the multiplying or dividing operations you can use to change these numbers. Try them on your calculator.

6 to 600	x 100	11 to 1.1	÷ 10
100 to 10	÷ 10	3 to 30	x 10
6.4 to 640	x 100	13.9 to 139	x 10
4.2 to 0.42	÷ 10	5.75 to 575	x 100
50 to 5000	x 100	8 to 0.08	÷ 100
29 to 2.9	÷ 10	50 to 0.5	÷ 100
8.6 to 86	x 10	47 to 470	x 10
530 to 5.3	÷ 100	6 to 0.6	÷ 10
2.9 to 29	x 10	4.16 to 416	x 100
1000 to 10	÷ 100	250 to 25	÷ 10

Decimals on a number line

You can show decimals on a number line. The arrow shows 1.3.

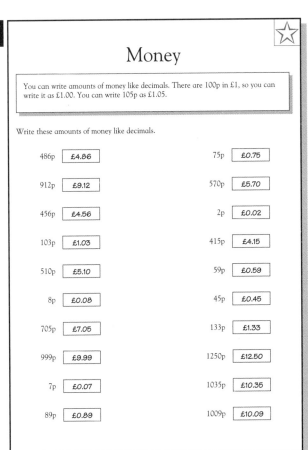

Draw arrows to show these decimals on the number lines.

0.3 and 1.5

0.9 and 1.7

0.7 and 1.4

0.8 and 1.9

Decimals on a number line

You can show hundredths as decimals on a number line. The arrow shows 1.15.

Draw arrows to show these decimals on the number lines.

1.4, 1.65 and 1.95

3.45, 3.55 and 3.8

5.3, 5.35 and 5.85

2.1, 2.25 and 2.75

Money

You can write amounts of money like decimals. There are 100p in £1, so you can write it as £1.00. You can write 105p as £1.05.

Write these amounts of money like decimals.

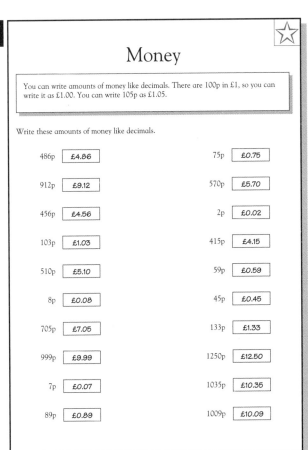

486p	£4.86	75p	£0.75
912p	£9.12	570p	£5.70
456p	£4.56	2p	£0.02
103p	£1.03	415p	£4.15
510p	£5.10	59p	£0.59
8p	£0.08	45p	£0.45
705p	£7.05	133p	£1.33
999p	£9.99	1250p	£12.50
7p	£0.07	1035p	£10.35
89p	£0.89	1009p	£10.09

Measurements as decimals

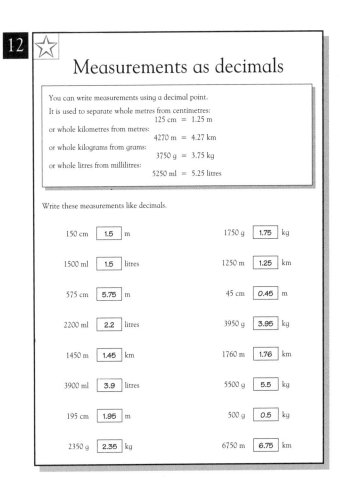

You can write measurements using a decimal point.

It is used to separate whole metres from centimetres:
125 cm = 1.25 m

or whole kilometres from metres:
4270 m = 4.27 km

or whole kilograms from grams:
3750 g = 3.75 kg

or whole litres from millilitres:
5250 ml = 5.25 litres

Write these measurements like decimals.

150 cm	1.5	m	1750 g	1.75	kg
1500 ml	1.5	litres	1250 m	1.25	km
575 cm	5.75	m	45 cm	0.45	m
2200 ml	2.2	litres	3950 g	3.95	kg
1450 m	1.45	km	1760 m	1.76	km
3900 ml	3.9	litres	5500 g	5.5	kg
195 cm	1.95	m	500 g	0.5	kg
2350 g	2.35	kg	6750 m	6.75	km

13

Rounding

When rounding decimals to the nearest whole number, numbers ending in 0.50 or more are *rounded up*. Numbers ending in 0.49 or less are *rounded down*.

2.48 rounds down to 2, and 3.75 rounds up to 4.

Round these decimals up or down to the nearest whole number.

4.29	4		7.86	8
6.57	7		59.45	59
7.43	7		42.71	43
18.2	18		91.93	92
52.1	52		62.78	63
8.85	9		13.64	14
9.01	9		26.01	26
5.63	6		35.55	36

14

Rounding

Round these amounts of money and measurements up or down to the nearest whole number.

£4.65	£5		8.65 kg	9 kg
5.35 kg	5 kg		£3.15	£3
£8.10	£8		6.3 m	6 m
7.75 cm	8 cm		2.85 m	3 m
5.89 cm	6 cm		£3.55	£4
£6.37	£6		9.45 kg	9 kg
5.25 kg	5 kg		4.1 m	4 m
£0.50	£1		8.88 kg	9 kg
6.05 cm	6 cm		£25.49	£25

15

Decimal equivalents

Write the decimal equivalents.

$\frac{8}{10}$ =	0.8		$\frac{4}{10}$ =	0.4
489p =	£4.89		35p =	£0.35
$\frac{1}{5}$ =	0.2		35 cm =	0.35 m
625 cm =	6.25 m		$\frac{4}{5}$ =	0.8
275p =	£2.75		150p =	£1.50
55 cm =	0.55 m		$\frac{1}{10}$ =	0.1
$\frac{2}{5}$ =	0.4		280 cm =	2.8 m
308p =	£3.08		16 cm =	0.16 m

16

Decimals from fractions

You will need a calculator.
To find a decimal from a fraction, you can divide the numerator by the denominator.
To find the decimal for $\frac{1}{10}$, divide 1 by 10 on the calculator.
The display should read 0.1

Use your calculator to find the decimal equivalents of these fractions. Write the divisions you can use.

	Division	Answer			Division	Answer
$\frac{1}{100}$ =	1 ÷ 100	= 0.01		$\frac{2}{10}$ =	2 ÷ 10	= 0.2
$\frac{25}{100}$ =	25 ÷ 100	= 0.25		$\frac{5}{100}$ =	5 ÷ 100	= 0.05
$\frac{49}{100}$ =	49 ÷ 100	= 0.49		$\frac{7}{10}$ =	7 ÷ 10	= 0.7
$\frac{3}{4}$ =	3 ÷ 4	= 0.75		$\frac{1}{4}$ =	1 ÷ 4	= 0.25
$\frac{1}{2}$ =	1 ÷ 2	= 0.5		$\frac{50}{100}$ =	50 ÷ 100	= 0.5
$\frac{10}{100}$ =	10 ÷ 100	= 0.1		$\frac{3}{60}$ =	3 ÷ 60	= 0.05

Making an estimate

Write whether you would estimate the following to the nearest 10, 100, 1000, 10 000, 100 000 or 1 000 000.

The number of insects on Earth.	1 000 000
The number of children in a class.	10
The number of shops in a town.	100 or 1000
The number of people watching a TV soap.	1 000 000
The number of spectators at an important football match.	10 000
The cost of a fleet of 15 cars (in pounds).	£1 000 000

Give examples, similar to those above, of something that you might estimate to the nearest: **Answers may vary**

10	people on a bus
100	words on a page
1000	trees in an orchard
10 000	people at a pop concert
100 000	books in a library
1 000 000	stars in the sky

Rounding to 100 and 1000

Round these numbers to the nearest 100 and then to the nearest 1000.

978	6829	3735
1000 1000	6800 7000	3700 4000

7511	2716	1008
7500 8000	2700 3000	1000 1000

Round the heights of these buildings to the nearest 100 cm.

12.76 m	36.17 m	22.98 m	18.22 m
1300 cm	3600 cm	2300 cm	1800 cm

Draw a ring around the option that shows the calculation in the box rounded to the nearest 1000.

1626 + 953	5443 – 3771
1500 + 1000	5500 – 3500
(2000 + 1000)	6000 – 4000
2500 + 900	(5000 – 4000)

Multiplying by 10

Multiply these decimals by 10.

0.25	2.5		3.14	31.4
1.75	17.5		15.27	152.7
5.56	55.6		156.35	1563.5

These statues are one tenth of their real heights. Write their real heights.

32.8 mm	44.5 mm	22.6 mm
328 mm	445 mm	226 mm

Multiply each number on the left by 10 and draw a line to join it to the correct answer on the right.

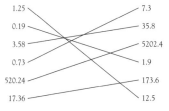

1.25	7.3
0.19	35.8
3.58	5202.4
0.73	1.9
520.24	173.6
17.36	12.5

Multiplying by 10 and 100

Multiply these decimals by 100.

6.25	625		3.14	314
11.75	1175		5.27	527
35.56	3556		1506.25	150 625

Write the missing numbers in the boxes.

0.06	0.6	6
101.1	1011	10 110
0.09	0.9	9
13.26	132.6	1326
3.145	31.45	314.5

Multiply each decimal on the left by 100 and draw a line to join it to the correct answer on the right.

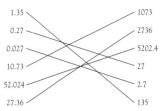

1.35	1073
0.27	2736
0.027	5202.4
10.73	27
52.024	2.7
27.36	135

21

Decimal notation

You can write a decimal in words.

For example, 1.123 is one and one tenth, two hundredths and three thousandths.

Write out these decimals in words.

3.517 | Three and five tenths, one hundredth and seven thousandths.

0.115 | One tenth, one hundredth and five thousandths.

1.023 | One and two hundredths and three thousandths.

16.002 | Sixteen and two thousandths.

4.448 | Four and four tenths, four hundredths and eight thousandths.

22

Decimal notation

Write the decimal equivalents for each of the following.

Three and six thousandths.
3.006

One tenth, three hundredths and seven thousandths.
0.137

Two tenths and five thousandths.
0.205

Fifteen and three tenths, one hundredth and six thousandths.
15.316

Nine tenths and nine thousandths.
0.909

Twelve and one thousandth.
12.001

23

One-step operations

You will need a calculator.
To change 2.5 to 25 in one operation you can do a multiplication.
$$2.5 \times 10 = 25$$
You can change 25 back to 2.5 by dividing.
$$25 \div 10 = 2.5$$
Similarly, you can change 2.5 to 250, and 250 back to 2.5 by multiplying and dividing by 100.

Write the one-step operation you can use to change these numbers. Try them on your calculator.

3.6 to 36   × 10   15.2 to 1.52   ÷ 10

4.8 to 480   × 100   250 to 2.5   ÷ 100

0.2 to 0.02   ÷ 10   0.01 to 1   × 100

330 to 3.3   ÷ 100   990 to 9.9   ÷ 100

5 to 0.05   ÷ 100   0.3 to 3   × 10

70 to 0.7   ÷ 100   5.5 to 550   × 100

24

One-step operations

You will need a calculator.
To continue the pattern 2, 2.5, 3, 3.5 and so on, you can do an addition.
$$2 + 0.5 = 2.5 \quad 2.5 + 0.5 = 3 \quad 3 + 0.5 = 3.5 \text{ and so on.}$$
So the one step needed to continue the pattern is to add 0.5 each time.

Use a calculator to work out the one-step operation you can use to continue these patterns. Write the step.

1.82, 1.84, 1.86 and so on
Add 0.02 each time.

0.09, 0.10, 0.11 and so on
Add 0.01 each time.

5, 0.5, 0.05 and so on
Divide by 10 each time.

0.16, 0.32, 0.64 and so on
Multiply by 2 each time.

1.55, 1.8, 2.05 and so on
Add 0.25 each time.

0.064, 0.128, 0.256 and so on
Multiply by 2 each time.

25 — Ordering decimals

Put these amounts in order from the largest to the smallest.

£3.56	£6.35	£3.65	£5.63	£5.36
£6.35	£5.63	£5.36	£3.65	£3.56

12.65 km	16.25 km	15.26 km	15.62 km	12.56 km
16.25 km	15.62 km	15.26 km	12.65 km	12.56 km

0.55 kg	0.09 kg	0.45 kg	0.54 kg	0.155 kg
0.55 kg	0.54 kg	0.45 kg	0.155 kg	0.09 kg

Put these amounts in order from the smallest to the largest.

106p	£1.60	£0.95	97p	£1.65
£0.95	97p	106p	£1.60	£1.65

1.35 m	110 cm	136 cm	1.53 m	1.01 m
1.01 m	110 cm	1.35 m	136 cm	1.53 m

1.25 litres	1200 ml	2.15 litres	1500 ml	1.56 litres
1200 ml	1.25 litres	1500 ml	1.56 litres	2.15 litres

26 — Converting

Convert these units.

2.125 km into m	2125 m
15.15 km into m	15 150 m
6.05 km into m	6050 m
7.005 km into m	7005 m
7.255 kg into g	7255 g
3.5 kg into g	3500 g
7.155 kg into g	7155 g
10.025 kg into g	10 025 g
1.25 litres into ml	1250 ml
10.25 litres into ml	10 250 ml
0.755 litres into ml	755 ml
1.055 litres into ml	1055 ml

27 — Decimals on a number line

Write the decimal each arrow is pointing to.

Draw arrows to show these decimals on the number line: 1.1, 2.7, 1.5, 2.9, 2.1

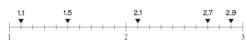

Write the decimal each arrow is pointing to.

Draw arrows to show these decimals on the number line: 1.05, 1.55, 1.8, 1.35, 1.9

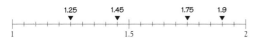

Write the decimal each arrow is pointing to.

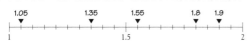
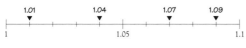

28 — Ordering decimals

Put these amounts in order from the largest to the smallest.

3.25	12.2	2.87	2.78	3.2
12.2	3.25	3.2	2.87	2.78

6.675	7.765	7.567	6.576	7.665
7.765	7.665	7.567	6.675	6.576

Put these amounts in order from the smallest to the largest.

1.75	1.57	2.05	2.15	2.005
1.57	1.75	2.005	2.05	2.15

16.681	18.616	16.816	18.661	18.166
16.681	16.816	18.166	18.616	18.661

Write the missing numbers to complete the sequences.

3.17	3.175	3.18
15.06	15.065	15.07
12.9	12.85	12.8
7.65	7.655	7.66
7.65	7.645	7.64

Word problems

	Answer	Working out
Add 2.3 litres and 450 ml.	2.75 litres	2.3 + 0.45 2.75
Add 375 ml and 5.25 litres.	5.625 litres	0.375 + 5.250 5.625
Subtract 255 g from 1.4 kg.	1.145 kg	1.400 − 0.255 1.145
Subtract 363 g from 2.59 kg.	2.227 kg	2.590 − 0.363 2.227

Solve these problems.

	Answer	Working out
A bag of nails weighs 1.25 kg and a small bag of screws weighs 225 g. What is the total weight of one bag of nails and two bags of screws?	1.7 kg	0.225 1.25 x 2 and + 0.45 0.450 1.70
Andrew weighed some dried beans. They weighed 1.63 kg. He took 325 g of beans off the scales. What was the weight of the remaining beans?	1.305 kg	1.630 − 0.325 1.305
A measuring jug contained 1.75 litres of water. Sarah poured in another 355 ml. How much water was in the measuring jug?	2.105 litres	1.750 + 0.355 2.105
Indu made 1.85 litres of soup in a saucepan and then poured out two bowls, each of which took 325 ml. How much soup is left in the saucepan?	1.2 litres	0.325 1.85 x 2 and − 0.65 0.650 1.20

Rounding

Round each decimal to the nearest whole number.

9.7	10	10.3	10
39.8	40	14.5	15
3.78	4	14.33	14
6.43	6	18.05	18
38.29	38	156.82	157
957.19	957	100.95	101
999.99	1000	101.01	101
9.09	9	110.11	110

Rounding

Round each decimal to the nearest tenth.

3.28	3.3	2.83	2.8
9.47	9.5	12.53	12.5
12.59	12.6	111.51	111.5
111.15	111.2	17.12	17.1
17.17	17.2	2.58	2.6
1.53	1.5	8.96	9
1.99	2	22.07	22.1
24.25	24.3	5.55	5.6
100.01	100	19.89	19.9

Equivalents

Write the fraction or decimal equivalents.

$^{7}/_{10}$	0.7
0.06	$^{6}/_{100}$ or $^{3}/_{50}$
0.003	$^{3}/_{1000}$
0.025	$^{25}/_{1000}$ or $^{1}/_{40}$
$^{17}/_{100}$	0.17
5.17	$5^{17}/_{100}$
6.25	$6^{25}/_{100}$ or $6^{1}/_{4}$
0.525	$^{525}/_{1000}$ or $^{21}/_{40}$
4.205	$4^{205}/_{1000}$ or $4^{41}/_{200}$
1.99	$1^{99}/_{100}$
1.09	$1^{9}/_{100}$
1.009	$1^{9}/_{1000}$
9.09	$9^{9}/_{100}$
9.99	$9^{99}/_{100}$